NASCAR Greats

Gail Blasser Riley
AR B.L.: 3.8
Points: 0.5   MG

BLAZERS®

The World of NASCAR

NASCAR Greats

by Gail Blasser Riley

Reading Consultant:
Barbara J. Fox
Reading Specialist
North Carolina State University

Content Consultant:
Betty L. Carlan
Research Librarian
International Motorsports Hall of Fame
Talladega, Alabama

Capstone
press®

Mankato, Minnesota

Blazers is published by Capstone Press,
151 Good Counsel Drive, P.O. Box 669, Mankato, Minnesota 56002.
www.capstonepress.com

Library of Congress Cataloging-in-Publication Data
Riley, Gail Blasser,
    NASCAR greats/by Gail Blasser Riley.
    p. cm. — (Blazers. The World of NASCAR)
    Includes bibliographical references and index.
    ISBN-13: 978-1-4296-1287-6 (hardcover)
    ISBN-10: 1-4296-1287-8 (hardcover)
    1. NASCAR (Association) — History — Juvenile literature. 2. Stock car
drivers — History — Juvenile literature. I. Title. II. Series.
GV1029.9.S74R547 2008
796.720922—dc22
[B]   2007022735

Summary: Describes the legends of NASCAR racing, including Richard Petty,
Dale Earnhardt, Cale Yarborough, and Darrell Waltrip.

Essential content terms are **bold** and are defined on the spread where they
first appear.

Editorial Credits
Mandy Robbins, editor; Bobbi J. Wyss, designer; Jo Miller, photo researcher

Photo Credits
AP Images, 15; Bob Jordon, 27; Lynne Sladky, cover (Richard Petty);
    Mark Foley, 7; Phil Coale, 8; Terry Renna, 12–13; Tom Strattman, 22
Corbis/Bettmann, 10, 19
DVIC/SRA Brian Ferguson, USAF, 20–21
Getty Images for NASCAR/Chris Trotman, 28–29; Jamie Squire, 25;
    Getty Images Inc./Allsport/Bill Hall, 16; David Taylor, 6, 24;
    Focus on Sport, 18
SportsChrome, Inc./Evan Pinkus, 5; Greg Crisp, cover (Dale Earnhardt), 9

1 2 3 4 5 6 13 12 11 10 09 08

Table of Contents

Success At Last 4

What Makes a Racer Great? 11

Legends 14

Today's Greats 23

Legendary Stats 20

Glossary 30

Read More 31

Internet Sites 31

Index 32

Success at Last

By 1998, Dale Earnhardt had
won 30 races at Daytona International
Speedway. But he had never won the
Daytona 500. On February 15, 1998,
he tried for the 20th time.

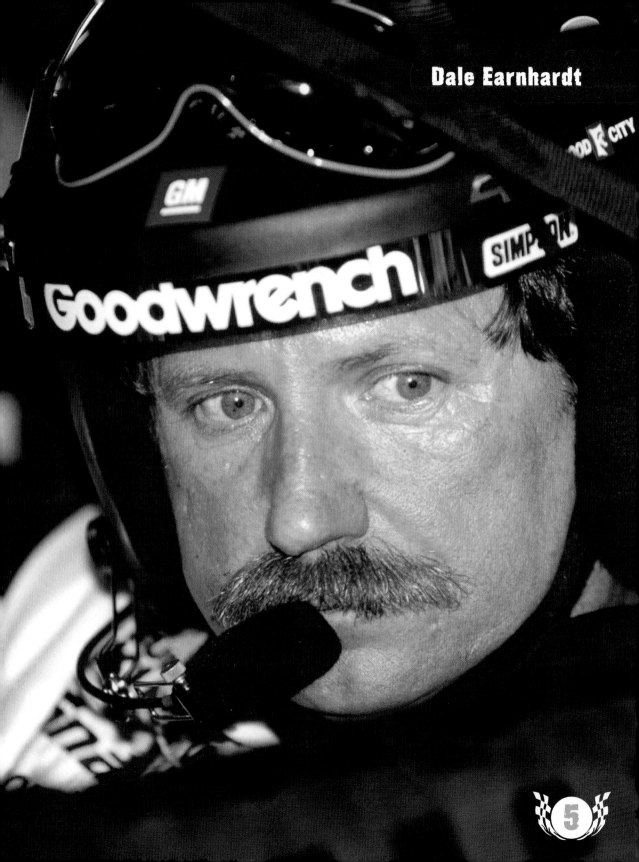

Dale Earnhardt

Earnhardt started in fourth place. He raced hard and left the last *pit stop* in first. Earnhardt had to keep his number 3 car in the lead for 26 more laps.

pit stop — when drivers take a break so the pit crew can add fuel, change tires, and make repairs

Jeremy Mayfield, Rusty Wallace, and Bobby Labonte were right behind Earnhardt. But he managed to hold them off.

taking the checkered flag

When the checkered flag waved,
Earnhardt was still in front. His 1998
Daytona 500 win helped make him
a NASCAR legend.

What Makes a Racer Great?

In the early days of NASCAR, racers sped around dirt tracks. The best drivers were daring, but smart.

2007, Daytona 500

Today, tracks are *paved*, and cars are faster. But the boldest and smartest drivers still find their way to the front.

paved — when a track is covered with a hard material like concrete or asphalt

TRACK FACT!

NASCAR greats Bill Elliott and Rusty Wallace took their love of speed to the sky. They both became pilots.

Legends

Richard Petty is called the King of NASCAR. He won 200 races and seven points championships. He was the first driver to earn $5 million.

TRACK FACT!

Richard Petty's father, Lee, won the first Daytona 500 in 1959.

15

Dale Earnhardt tied Petty's seven points championships. Earnhardt also earned more money than any other driver.

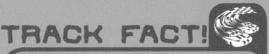

TRACK FACT!

Sadly, Dale Earnhardt died when his car crashed during the 2001 Daytona 500.

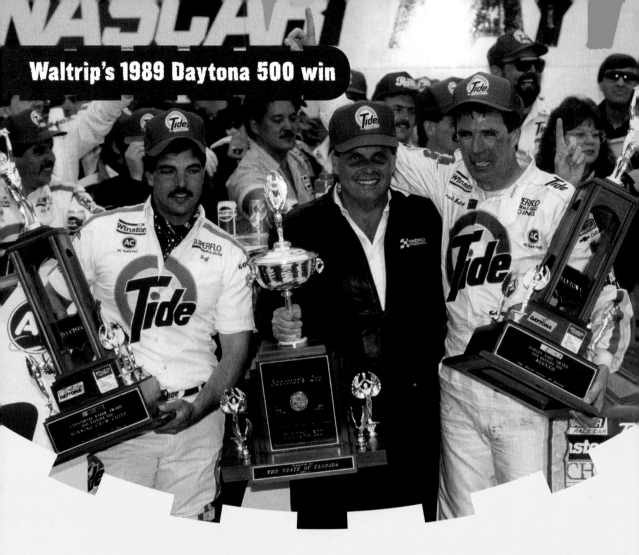

Darrell Waltrip lit up the NASCAR scene in the 1980s. He won the points championship three times. He also won the Daytona 500 in 1989.

Cale Yarborough raced in NASCAR for about 30 years. He is the only driver to win three points championships in a row.

Yarborough's 1977 Daytona 500 win

19

Legendary Stats

Lee Petty
Most popular car #: 42 **Time span:** 1949–1964
Championships: 3 **Total wins:** 54

Buck Baker
Most popular car #: 87 **Time span:** 1949–1976
Championships: 2 **Total wins:** 46

Joe Weatherly
Most popular car #: 8 **Time span:** 1952–1964
Championships: 2 **Total wins:** 25

Cale Yarborough
Most popular car #: 11 **Time span:** 1957–1988
Championships: 3 **Total wins:** 83

Richard Petty
Most popular car #: 43 **Time span:** 1958–1992
Championships: 7 **Total wins:** 200

David Pearson

Most popular car #: 21 **Time span:** 1960–1986
Championships: 3 **Total wins:** 105

Bobby Allison

Most popular car #: 12 & 22 **Time span:** 1961–1988
Championships: 1 **Total wins:** 85

Darrell Waltrip

Most popular car #: 17 **Time span:** 1972–2000
Championships: 3 **Total wins:** 83

Dale Earnhardt

Most popular car #: 3 **Time span:** 1975–2001
Championships: 7 **Total wins:** 76

Bill Elliot

Most popular car #: 9 **Time span:** 1976–2007
Championships: 1 **Total wins:** 44

21

Gordon's 2004 Brickyard 400 win

Today's Greats

By the end of 2006, Jeff Gordon had won four championships. He was half way to beating the record shared by Petty and Earnhardt.

Tony Stewart has raced almost everything on wheels. He hit the *Sprint Cup* scene in 1999. Stewart won three races that year. By 2005, he had won two points championships.

Sprint Cup — NASCAR's top stock car racing series

Stewart racing an Indy car

TRACK FACT!

Stewart started racing go-karts when he was 7 years old.

In 1998, Matt Kenseth finished sixth in his first Sprint Cup race. He won the points championship five years later.

NASCAR
Winston Cup
Series

2003
NASCAR WINSTON CUP CHAMPION
MATT KENSETH

Kenseth's 2003 points championship

Top drivers also include Jimmie Johnson, Kurt Busch, and Dale Earnhardt Jr. These great drivers keep fans coming back for more.

NASCAR's top ten drivers of 2006

TRACK FACT!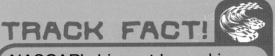

NASCAR's biggest legend is "Big" Bill France. He helped form NASCAR in 1947.

Glossary

checkered flag (CHEK-urd FLAG) — a flag with a pattern of black and white squares, used to signal when the first car has crossed the finish line

paved (PAYVED) — when a road or sidewalk is covered with a hard material such as concrete or asphalt

pit stop (PIT STOP) — a break drivers take from the race so the pit crew can add fuel, change tires, and make repairs to a car

points champion (POINTS CHAM-pee-uhn) — the driver who earns the most points in a NASCAR racing season; drivers earn points for where they finish in a race.

Sprint Cup (SPRINT CUP) — the prize received for winning the points championship in NASCAR's top stock car racing series; it is also the name of the series; from 2004 to 2007, it was called the Nextel Cup; from 1972 through 2003, it was called the Winston Cup; before 1972, it was known as the Grand National.

Read More

Armentrout, David and Patricia. *Tony Stewart.* In the Fast Lane. Vero Beach, Fla.: Rourke, 2007.

Kelley, K. C. *Daring Drivers: If You Were a NASCAR Driver.* All-Star Readers. Pleasantville, N.Y.: Reader's Digest, 2005.

Schaefer, A. R. *Richard Petty.* NASCAR Racing. Mankato, Minn.: Capstone Press, 2007.

Internet Sites

FactHound offers a safe, fun way to find Internet sites related to this book. All of the sites on FactHound have been researched by our staff.

Here's how:
1. Visit *www.facthound.com*
2. Choose your grade level.
3. Type in this book ID **1429612878** for age-appropriate sites. You may also browse subjects by clicking on letters, or by clicking on pictures and words.
4. Click on the **Fetch It** button.

FactHound will fetch the best sites for you!

Index

Busch, Kurt, 28

championships, 14, 17, 18, 19, 23, 24, 26
checkered flag, 8

Daytona 500, 4, 6–8, 14, 17, 18

Earnhardt, Dale, 4, 6–8, 17, 23
Earnhardt, Dale Jr., 28
earnings, 14, 17
Elliott, Bill, 13

fans, 28

Gordon, Jeff, 23

Johnson, Jimmie, 28

Kenseth, Matt, 26

Labonte, Bobby, 7

Mayfield, Jeremy, 7

Petty, Lee, 14
Petty, Richard, 14, 17, 23
pit stops, 6

records, 14, 17, 23

Sprint Cup. *See* championships
statistics, 20–21
Stewart, Tony, 24, 25

tracks, 11–13
Daytona International Speedway, 4

Wallace, Rusty, 7, 13
Waltrip, Darrell, 18

Yarborough, Cale, 19